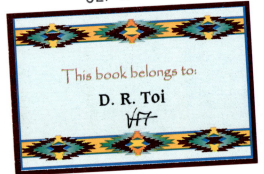

BEING ESSENCE

Keys to The Kingdom

Jasmuheen

Self Empowerment Academy
P.O. Box 1754
Buderim 4556
Queensland Australia
Fax: +61 7 5445 6075
www.selfempowermentacademy.com.au
www.jasmuheen.com

Published August 2012

*Please respect the work of the author
& help S.E.A. promote planetary peace.*

For copies as an e-Book go to:
http://www.jasmuheen.com/products-page/

For copies as a Hardcover book go to:
http://www.lulu.com/spotlight/jasmuheen

ESSENCE IS

Essence is the All That Is,
Supreme in Its attendance.
Essence is pure love in waves,
powerful in transcendence.
Essence holds the path of peace,
the way of stepping forward.
Essence flows behind the scenes
then calls us all toward It.
Essence sings a song so pure
for open hearts to listen.
Essence fills us from our core,
then radiates and glistens.
Essence feeds us through our soul,
It fills us with great wonder.
Essence is creation's core,
upon which, the wise, do ponder.

CONTENTS

Introduction
Our Books of Being

1. Essence
2. Our Essence in form on Earth
3. Realities
4. Our Essence and Our Illusionary Selves
5. Identification
6. Keys to the Kingdom
7. BEing Essence

Our Baseline Essence
Our Paradise – additional Kingdom Keys
- Law of Love plus Meditation
- Prayer Power, Prayer Time
- Peace & Paradise Codes
- Perfect Communication
- Three Level Guidance System
- Breath Test Guidance plus meditation
- B.E. - Baseline Essence Meditation

Our Essence as Cosmic Micro Food
The Tribe of I AM

Introduction

Like others I meet these days, I live my life in a state of deep peace and contentment; my heart's prayer is one of constant gratitude and my soul is full of music and song. The journey to get to this place has been long yet extremely interesting – at least to me.

After nearly forty years of meditation, nearly twenty years of being physically nourished by prana plus eighteen years of constant travel all around this world, my personal rhythm in life has stabilised into a state of feeling blessed and graced, nourished, well loved and supported. My life feels rich in quality and my heart even richer again.

During this time I have also had the joy and the profound learning of raising a family, seeing three grandchildren come into this world and developing close and loving relationships with friends and my husband-lover of the last few decades.

Through all of this I have faced so many challenges, as we all do in life especially as our loved ones leave to transition on to other planes and yet each major life challenge delivered virtues that I obviously needed to help fulfil a long held goal.

At seven years of age, this goal was to discover and dwell in the Kingdom of Heaven that Jesus spoke of in the Bible. Later this goal changed to an interest in ascension, becoming enlightened; for by age sixteen the Indian Mahatmas had entered my life, carrying an energy that I sensed that I desired. They were peaceful, wise, gentle and loving beings who radiated something that I didn't know I yearned for until I felt it coming from them. Via daily satsang, they shared of the wonders of the realms we can discover when we turn our senses inward.

The day they taught me to meditate was a turning point in my life, my biggest 'Aha' moment and one never to be forgotten. Using the ancient Vedic techniques, my third eye, then my body exploded in a starburst of light, dissolving me completely into it. And with this light came love, pure and profound, a love so divine it freed me of all hunger.

In those few moments I was fully enlightened and free, for in that experience I found that I was my Enlightened Essence. Somewhere deep inside me was a pure and perfect, loving and wise being that unfortunately retreated back deeper inside after those few glorious moments of revelation, leaving me completely addicted to all that It brought to my naïve and very young being.

An experience like that cannot be described or walked away from for our Essence is the most seductive, perfect lover.

When It rises It fills every cell, flowing through every atom of our Being from the dimension in which It resides within us all. It is the very fabric of our Being, It breathes us and lovingly gives expression to all life. All kingdoms, all dimensions exist based in this Essence which is the underlying frequency of all of creation.

Spoken of, and experienced by all of our Holy Ones, the rising of our Essence is an art to be learnt. Yet there are many pathways to be played with, for it all is just a blending and merging of rhythms that we carry until this rhythm delivers us to the kingdom of our choice.

And thankfully the Kingdom of Heaven has its doors of entry, for it exists as a frequency, a song deep within us that can be released for us to live in when we match with its harmonic.

After writing 35 books that are in 18 languages, for the last few years my focus has been on providing free information through the hundreds of videos we now have on our YouTube channel as so many now enjoy the modality of short educational and entertaining videos.

Yet one morning as I lay in the dreamtime, just before fully waking to a sun-filled sky in the sacred city of Sophia in Bulgaria, my head was full of guidance to again put pen to paper and write this book, and simplify again the things that we have shared for so long in so many ways in this world.

In this manual we share simple yet profound truths that will also bring the Breatharian reality in a deeper, clearer perspective. We will also offer simple techniques for the creation and revelation of the 'Paradise – Kingdom of Heaven' type realms.

Yet in Essence it is all about our Essence, for it is our Enlightened Essence that gives us this freedom to be nourished on all levels, in such a different way. And when a human being is well nourished from deep within by their Essence, then they too radiate this pure nourishment wherever they go, wherever they are and so our world transforms itself into the Garden of Eden that it too, was always destined to be.

I dedicate this book to the Christed Ones and to the Mahatmas of India who lovingly bestowed me with the tools to experience

Jai Sat Chit Ananda –
Truth, consciousness and bliss.

May we all enjoy our own Enlightened Essence and walk Its peace-filled pathways!

Jasmuheen

Our Books of Being

Like many, I feel as if I have completed a whole "book of being", filled with chapters of change and revelation; of self knowledge and the joyous journey of discovery of the various harmonics in life.

This includes the harmonics of self refinement and the gifts this brings as we are then magnetised through so many new realms and dimensions in the matrix of creation; it also includes the harmonics of family and community life; the harmonics of being one people on one planet; the harmonics of true tantra or Oneness in relationship to a lover and also the joy that this brings as our romantic relationship goes into higher and purer levels of expression; plus all the other streams of energy we can develop and be harmonized into.

The reason I say that my "book of being" is complete is that making the experiential shift to unity consciousness creates a whole new book of life experience for it is a completely different paradigm to all that we have known on Earth before which has usually been a duality based experience.

Perhaps our "Books of Being" are like a series, each one complete in themselves and each one a chapter of a much greater book again – a book that appears to have no beginning and no end.

The "Book of Being" in Unity Consciousness obviously runs by the same universal rules and laws as all books, however the mindset within unity consciousness is very different to what we have experienced on Earth before when we played our games of judgement and separation.

One of the dominant frequencies in the book of being in unity consciousness is allowance – total acceptance of the "Isness" and perfection of everything and the allowance for all to unfold around us as it needs to, free from any judgement of right or wrong.

We all know that we have a common baseline frequency upon which our own unique experiences weave or leave an imprint. We call this baseline frequency our Essence, the I AM that I AM pure energy that supports all of creation. Perhaps we understand that yes, we are all cells in a divine body of being, part of one vibrating mass of Beingness, an idea that we experience when we meditate and feel our Essence deep within with its pulse of love and wisdom.

Translating this to a non-judgemental state of allowance takes this idea into an experiential truth of true unity consciousness. For me this translation happened over a few days during a visit into India awhile ago and was triggered by an "Ahha" moment insight.

At the Global Congress of Spiritual Scientists (GCSS), one of the speakers had been talking to the group about how we are all just like fingernails on the hand of a giant, how when we are unaware of who we truly are and when we identify too much with our physical structure, we tend to think that the totality of our being is just our existence as the fingernail.

Yet when we meditate and feel our Essence and identify with our Essence instead, our consciousness expands and we see that we are not just the fingernail but we are the finger, the hand and the whole body.

While the speaker's talk was different to this and his focal point was more about the intelligence of the whole Beingness as being far greater than that of the fingernail, the analogy sat well with the group and later led to many discussions.

For me I realised yet again that this divine Beingness, this Essence that supports us all, has elected to have many unique expressions within the flow of creation. For example, obviously the experience of being the fingernail on the middle finger is different to being the fingernail on the little finger and both are different again to the experience of being the bone or the knuckle of the finger.

I began to see that people I love are also just like little fingernails that need to have their own unique experience as part of this body of Beingness and hence they are also a member of the whole I AM tribe, where the idea of tribe represents all the unique expressions the vast I AM consciousness is taking as unique physical extensions of its own Beingness.

In this understanding it is so obvious that firstly every life-form is just a slightly different expression of our own I AM, and each one has its own unique formula of experience that is perfect for it.

Hence there is no need to judge and every requirement is for us to just accept. For example, if someone that we care about is choosing a potentially short life, peppered with experiences for example, of living in an alcoholic haze, then it is wonderful that they – as an expression of our I AM Essence – can have this experience for us. They would not have set this experience up for themselves if it did not have value for them on some level and they cannot come out of this experience until they are ready and their learning is done.

Separation consciousness is maintained when we judge ourselves or each other as not being in the perfect rhythm that we believe that we or others should be in because we still see and judge each other as separate.

Yet who is in control anyway? Surely our I AM Essence in all its wisdom knows what sort of experience we need to have in all realms?

And because our Essence is the very baseline frequency within creation, then everything expressed from this Essence is an aspect of an energy we all are part of. Everything is just us having a unique experience that adds to the whole and so all is perfect.

Somehow in India I got this on another deeper level and so I let go. Within an instant so much in my life changed and it really felt as if my whole book of being, of separatist thinking within the dual natured worlds, was complete. And with this pure acceptance and allowance, everything around me was set free.

In this expanded state of awareness I can feel how I exist as this endless Beingness, a pure Essence that permeates everything and how just a drop of this Essence is within a physical structure that I call my life on Earth today.

The beauty of our Essence or 'I AM' awareness is that we can travel unhindered through the matrix of creation, moving as pure thought faster than the speed of light, to focus on any aspect of this divine beingness that calls us. In this reality flow, there is no limit and no restriction except if we believe there is.

We all have so many amazing experiences in our dream life, in meditations, and sometimes from using various shamanic tools and also just by going through the myriad of challenges we have faced in our lives by identifying too much with our physical being structure and not enough with our Essence, the energy that keeps a body alive. For so long we have accepted so many limited realities that come with duality consciousness until we can learn what is needed and expand out from this into a more unified field.

In the unified field we truly are happy for all the experiences each life-form has chosen to have, for we know that each adds unique flavours to the whole that we all can experience and gain benefit from as we open to the Oneness flow.

Through this letting go of judgement of others also comes the letting go of judgement of ourselves, for we realise that while a drop of our Essence is having a human experience right here right now, this same Essence self as the I AM that I AM is having a multitude of simultaneous experiences throughout the matrix - being Elohim as the architects of creation, being Angels who obey Divine Will, being Ascended Ones as Light Beings, being extraterrestrials in all their flavours, being elements and elementals, or just imbuing universes as cosmic plasma flows. The list is as endless as our imagination and yes we are doing it all simultaneously here, now.

And in this light we can relax and just enjoy this human expression for all that being human contains – loving the fact that we have bodies, loving the fact that we have our seven senses with which to enjoy all realms including this dense physical plane of Earth.

Right here, right now, I can breathe deep and slow to match the rhythm of my I AM Essence as it breathes through me without effort. In its rhythm there is only peace and deep contentment.

Right here, right now, I can close my eyes and let my awareness expand out from my physical form to flow like cosmic plasma, fluid and free, going any where through any dimension that my frequency can match with and then flow into.

Right here, right now, I can feel appreciation for every life-form in our vast I AM tribe, acknowledging and treasuring the experience that each life-form is gathering back into the whole.

To be this truth, to feel it and not just know about it; this too brings so much freedom as we feel and sense, experience and know, the perfection of it all.

So it is and so it always has been.

~1~
ESSENCE

- Our Essence Is.
- It contains creation.
- It sustains creation.
- It is pure light.
- It is pure love.
- It is pure sound.
- In its light, love and sound are all the blueprints and patterns for creation.
- Its patterns and blueprints hold infinite wisdom and infinite fields of potential.
- It is pure joy.
- It is pure bliss
- And yet ... it is much more again.
- It is the nameless, the formless,
- the void that defies explanation.
- We are its dream.
- We are its reality.
- We are all extensions of Essence, lovingly connected as part of the pattern of its weave.
- We are multiple, unique versions of this Essence in form.
- As Essence in form, we too are creator Gods, for the Essence within us holds all the keys to the blueprints of creation.
- As Essence in form we too can weave any pattern we desire for we have the free will to do this.
- Our Enlightened Essence is just one of many rhythms we hold within our Earth-bound energy system that we call a body,
- and yet we, as pure Essence, exist multi-dimensionally way beyond this physical world.
- We are infinite in our true nature.
- We are eternal in our true expression.

Mantra of Essence Reclamation

I AM LOVE
I AM ETERNAL
I AM INFINITE

Chant the above with sincerity over and over when you are in the peaceful rhythm of meditation or whenever you need to remind yourself as to who you really are.

Meditate on the attributes that you feel your own pure Essence expresses. The more we focus on Being Essence, the more aligned to It we become.

Brief Meditation using the above Mantra:-

- Take a few minutes to slow your breathing rhythm right down
- As you slowly chant *I AM* on the inhale and *LOVE* on the exhale
- Imagine also that you are drawing through your atoms, from the highest dimensions within, pure Essence energy.
- Imagine exhaling this pure Essence energy and filling every cell with Its nourishing flow.
- With this slow, deep and refined breathing rhythm and the above intention keep slowly chanting the mantra *I AM LOVE* and feel, sense how your body is responding to this.
- Next keeping this same slow breathing rhythm and intention that
- you are drawing through your atoms, from the highest dimensions within, pure Essence energy.
- Then again imagine exhaling this pure Essence energy and filling every cell with Its nourishing flow.
- Now change the mantra to slowly chant *I AM* on the inhale
- With the slow chant of *ETERNAL* on the exhale.
- Stay with this for a few moments and again just be aware of how your system is responding.
- Then when you are ready change the chant to *I AM INFINITE.*

This breathing rhythm of intention, plus the chants, is designed to align your cellular structure more powerfully to your Essence energy.

~2~
OUR ESSENCE IN FORM ON EARTH

- Just one small drop of our Enlightened Essence is expressed in our body on Earth.
- As Essence we exist in all realms simultaneously
- and so we can explore and enjoy all of our Essence expressions, for we are not bound to these bodies or to this earthly plane.
- As such we are multiversal, inter-dimensional beings who carry all the rhythms of the universes within.
- As a system of energy we hold unique physical, emotional, mental and spiritual rhythms.
- These rhythms change moment to moment.
- Our total bio-system rhythm is a mix, a blend of our ever-changing physical, emotional, mental and spiritual rhythms.
- This blended rhythm is our personal energy signature,
- it is how the quantum field and the U.F.I. – the Universal Field of Infinite Love and Intelligence – respond to us.
- Hence our personal energy harmonic or signature is constantly creating our reality via the Universal Law of Resonance.

Mantra for a perfected energy signature

"I exist in the rhythm of health, happiness and harmony
on all levels within myself and with all life."

Say the above with sincerity, trusting that the intelligent
universe will support you to bring this into truth.

Support the universal Essence flows
by also living the day to day lifestyle
– that we discuss later –
to help create this truth.

~3~
REALITIES

- There are multiple realities.
- Everyone perceives reality through their emotional, mental and spiritual body conditioning and filters.

There is also:-
- The pure reality of our Enlightened Essence, and also
- the various illusionary realities that we create when we live too far away from the perfected rhythm of our Essence and identify too much with our external plane three dimensional world.
- Our Essence is our baseline frequency, the fabric on which we draw the pattern of our life.

With a sincere heart, in meditation, ask to experience the reality of your Essence in such a profound way that is perfect for you, so that you will never again doubt, or be unaware of Its' love, wisdom and power.

Ask to experience all Its' gifts and all the glories that It holds for you.

Glory Days

I have all I need and more,
such abundance at my door,
a heart that's never poor,
there's all I need and more.

Yes all I have is true,
since I discovered you,
this Essence that's so pure,
It's light and laughter too.

And so I sing this praise,
for now there's glory days,
a joy in love's true ways,
a freedom we'd long craved.

~4~
OUR ESSENCE and
OUR ILLUSIONARY SELVES

- Living in duality and the third dimensional realms while still containing OUR ENLIGHTENED ESSENCE and being breathed by It, means we constantly create and then relate to, many versions of ourselves.
- Our bio-systems can be likened to a grand piano, whose keyboard holds many notes or octaves of expression.
- Our highest note, the most refined frequency is the octave of Our Enlightened Essence energy pool.
- The lowest, deepest note is like the version of ourselves that has been educated to believe it is just a physical, emotional and mental body system. This version is often unaware of the internal Essence energy pool it carries.
- All of these octaves exist as a spiralling flow of energy within us.
- At the top of the spiral, we exist in the outer world of duality, relating to and governed by our personality self.
- This is the world of illusion, of reflections of our thinking, feeling and lifestyle patterns.
- This is the part of us that has been formed by genetic, family, cultural, plus educational, past and current timeline experiences; it is our ego-based nature.
- At the other end of the spiral deep within us, is the Kingdom of Heaven that Jesus spoke of, Buddha's Pure Land, Mohammed's Paradise World where our Enlightened Essence resides in full force – powerful, wise and loving.
- Here our Essence is like a central heating system whose flame burns bright and pure.
- At the top end of the spiral, our Essence can still be felt or we would not have life, however it resides within the personality energy pool in a more diluted form, as here the octave or note of the personality self is more dominant.
- Conversely in the realm of the pure Essence, the personality self is one small drop in the vast ocean of Essence.

- This spiralling flow of energy is constantly flowing like wind through a tunnel, where each atom is the tunnel through which our Essence flows from the purest dimensions we carry within.
- This Essence energy comes directly from the Great Central Sun of the highest dimensions within.
- Every human system carries every octave and dimension of expression overlaid within it and the octave of expression that we most identify with is always the most influential.
- Access to these octaves is through our atoms which Nassim Haramein's science has proven to be black holes.
- Our brain wave patterns and total bio-system resonance also determines which dimensions we can access and dwell in – both within and around us.

In You It Abides

There once was a wise man,
who sang from his heart,
yes there once was a wise man
who sang of light's path.
He called all the people to his mountain top,
he said, "Sit awhile, relax now, just stop,
for the Kingdom of Heaven in you it abides,
so he said, just sit still and feel love's sweet ride."

There once was a woman, who sang sweet and true,
whoever she touched, would see what was pure.
She said, "Come my children and rest deep inside
for love that is true, in you, it abides.
So be still and just listen and open your heart,
and then you will know that you are but a part,
of something so grand and something so pure,
yes the Kingdom of Heaven abides within you."

There once was a wise man,
who sang from his heart,
yes, there once was a woman
and she played her part.

Yes, this Kingdom of Heaven, they say this is true,
that this Kingdom of Heaven abides now in you,
a Kingdom of Heaven, in me, and in you.

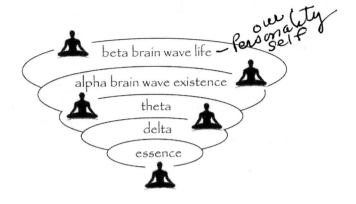

~5~
IDENTIFICATION

- As a fluid, ever changing energy system we can identify with all the different versions of ourselves to create and enjoy any reality we choose.
- **Identification solely with our personality self**, keeps our brain wave patterns in busy Beta frequency mode.
- Here the physical body needs nourishment from physical food or it will die.
- Here we stay subject to the usual experiences we have as humans in a dense three dimensional - 3D - realm where polarity is seen as normal.
- Here it is considered 'normal' for people to be victims, get sick, age and die from disease or old age.
- With sole identification with our personality self version, life has its ups and downs.
- In this energy version we are often easily influenced by external forces, reacting to what occurs in life in positive or negative ways.
- As our personality selves, we are also greatly influenced by the genetic weaknesses we may carry and by the fact we are continually altering our DNA and genetic patterns via traumas, thoughts and toxins - as cellular biologist Dr Bruce Lipton has explained in his work *"The Biology of Belief"*.
- With this level of identification we experience many human limitations that are associated with living a normal mainstream life.

- As we apply what we call the 'KEYS TO THE KINGDOM' in the next chapter, our brain wave patterns shift to a different system of operation, from Beta to Alpha to Theta to Delta.
- With the Keys applied and the changing of our brain wave patterns, we move also from being governed by subconscious behaviour patterns, to more conscious mind patterns, to operating in super conscious reality streams where our lower mental plane abilities merge with the Divine or Supreme mind of our Enlightened Essence nature.
- Here telepathy and divine communion with Beings of Light becomes the norm,
- as does third eye activation for our clairvoyant abilities to surface, along with the rising of our clairsentient nature.
- In this new system of operation we find ourselves less hungry for anything in the material world.
- As we identify more with the versions of ourselves that dwell closer to the fire of our Essence nature, we also find that we naturally become less physically hungry.
- As these versions are more infused with the purer more complex element mix of our Essence, we are freed from emotional, mental and spiritual hungers as well.
- Hence with this level of identification and with a more constant Theta-Delta brain wave pattern, the physiology of our system changes.
- As we relate more to, and are more closely aligned to, the versions of ourselves that are more infused with Essence, we find that our emotional and mental rhythms are more peaceful, contented;
- More imbued with Essence we also find that we feel more gratitude, compassion and appreciation.
- We also realize that we can be anywhere and be unaffected by this world in an adverse way as long as we choose to radiate out our pure Essence rather than absorb the energies from the external plane around us.
- Aligned to our Essence nature, in this rhythm we tend to see the God in all and the Good in all.
- In this rhythm our life is harmonic as are our interactions with everyone else.
- Here our life is filled with Grace as the universe tends to serve us as we naturally serve others.

- Here we live in a field of abundance, an abundance of love, clarity, wisdom, vision
- and here everything we need is delivered to us before we realise we may need it.

I like the version of myself that is most imbued with Essence yet like many I can shift in an instant into other versions as well. While I no longer dwell solely as my personality self, I can still find sadness in life as I continually let go of my limited human conditioning.

Opening to unity consciousness teaches us many new ways of Being. To understand that those we love are also extensions of our own Essence, whose journey on Earth is also unique and to let them go and live their own journeys, is also an art.

To love all unconditionally, to trust that the Essence in all is guiding all, even though it may not appear to be, is also a path of trust, of learning to let go of judgement, of ideas of right or wrong and to see all life as just different layers of expressions of Essence.

While some people appear lost or confused, sad or lonely and hence our compassionate heart can feel their pain and wish to help, everyone's journey delivers so many gifts to us all, as we each must find the keys to the Kingdom of a Heaven of our own creation, if that is what we truly desire.

- We may also need to accept that not everyone desires now to experience this inner heavenly Kingdom,
- and that some people on Earth are young souls who need to be immersed in the game of duality for a while.
- Hence, to lovingly allow each flower to grow and blossom in its own way and time, is also an art to learn.

Exercise:- Train yourself to see the God in all and the good in all.

Spend at least a week focused fully on this exercise until it is a truth for you and you can go beyond the more limited superficial appearances of first impressions.

Begin this exercise by firstly looking deeper and deeper into yourself, as you stand before a mirror, until you can see how your Essence is always shining out through your eyes.

Ask to see existence and your life through the eyes of your Essence.

Then look to see the shining light of Essence in the eyes of all you meet.

~6~
KEYS TO THE KINGDOM

Essence is also our Zen Master Self ...

Many in the busyness of Western world life never take the time to find their Zen-master self who is easily attuned to the now, the one who lives in a peaceful river of deep contentment within us. Our Zen-master self is a part of ourselves that lives closer to the level of our essence, for sometimes there is such a huge distance between our personality selves and the essence that breathes us and gives us life. Bridging this distance is the path of the spiritual initiate, a path that begins to reveal itself to those who long for peace or as soon as a human being begins to tire of the limitations of this external world.

Yet this path also has so many variations and detours along the way. Sometimes we sit with a guru for a while in hope to be imbued by some of their radiance or wisdom, before finally realising that we must be our own guru and more fully express the guru within which is our Essence nature.

Then we have the discovery of an infinite flow of love and wisdom that is bubbling deep within, ready to rise out of our own baseline essence as soon as we focus upon it and live the appropriate lifestyle to match frequencies with it, as is the way of the fields.

I love the science of life that drives all of our creations allowing metaphysics to have logic as Universal Laws control the flows and what we manage to manifest.

Sometimes it is our karma to manifest great riches yet the spiritual initiate soon realises that to be truly rich one must remember once more and BE who they truly are. In the inner realms material wealth holds no power for here true wealth is purity of heart and a sincere desire to operate in a way that serves the greater good. These are keys to kingdoms deep within us where true riches can be found.

In this chapter we now wish to share some of the main Keys that many have now used to find the Kingdom of Heaven within them and thus exist on Earth as if it truly is the prophesised Garden of Eden that we now know it is destined to be.

Key 1
Universal Laws

- Understand and apply in life, three Universal Laws.
- The Law of One, The Law of Love and The Law of Attraction also known as The Law of Resonance.

- **The Law of Love** states that divine love, as the original force of creation, has the power to transmute everything it touches back into its original form.
- Hence we can commit our lives to the service of being a cosmic transmission station through which divine love constantly radiates.
- As it moves through us flowing in from the inner universes through the atoms of our Being, it nourishes us, frees and transforms us before flowing out through the pores of our skin to touch and infuse others who are open to this love.

- **The Law of One** states that as we all share the same Essence and are hence interconnected in the web of life, everything we are and do affects the whole.
- Knowing this, then the act of self-mastery requires us to be responsible for all our energy emanations.
- With this we are invited to use the following mantra and say it out loud three times with sincere hearted intention:
- "Everything about my Beingness enhances this world and everything about this world enhances my Beingness. I open for Essence guidance so that this may be truth."
- You may wish to restate the above mantra anytime that you feel yourself being too judgmental about this world or when you are feeling too separate from others as this mantra is designed to bring us into a new system of operation.

- **The Law of Resonance** states that energy extends itself out to then attract like frequencies and return to its Source of creation. Hence the universe as we see it is just a reflection of our own energy transmissions which are an extension of our own consciousness.

See more on these laws at our YouTube channel under our Universal Harmonization Playlist.
  - Universal Laws:- Part 1; Part 2; Part 3; Part 4.

Also to experience more of The Law of Love, do the Love Breath Meditation daily at this link:-
http://www.youtube.com/watch?v=04j0ZmP6jEg&feature=plcp

Key 2
Lifestyle, lifestyle, lifestyle!

How we choose to spend our time determines our bio-system emanations and how the U.F.I. and quantum field reacts to us.

After 18 years of research we have found that nearly all people who successfully feed themselves physically by their Essence, plus many of those who dwell in what they feel is their paradise world, have spent their time involved in the below 8 points.

We call this **The Luscious Lifestyles Program**.

1. Meditation - where our intention is to experience our Essence and open to its gifts.
2. Prayer or Divine Communion – talking to the U.F.I. (Universal Field of Infinite love and intelligence) as if it is our best friend.
3. Positive thinking and mind mastery – understanding the power of thought and clear intention in reality creation.
4. A light diet – eat light-filled foods, live food with lots of life force and eat less. "Live, light and less" is the new food mantra.
5. Treat the body as a temple – give it lots of love and fun exercise that it enjoys.
6. Selfless service – be kind and compassionate to all life, help others when required without thought of personal reward.
7. Silence – be in silence at home and in nature for silence allows us to hear the voice of our Essence.
8. Sing sacred music and listen to it as well, as this is nourishment for our hearts and emotional body.

The Luscious Lifestyles Program – L.L.P. – has been designed to create fitness on all levels of our being regardless of our culture and religion. Based on Biofield Science principles, this holistic lifestyle improves health and happiness levels, increases our mental clarity and intuitive capacities, stimulates the expression of our Divine nature and makes us more compassionate, altruistic people. How we choose to spend our time is the key to loving life!

> Francois Voltaire, French philosopher and author, said "I decided to be happy because it is healthy."

All of the above has been discussed in detail in <u>The Food of Gods</u> book.

It is the combination of the above that shifts both our brain wave patterns from busy Beta through to Alpha and Theta, and allows us to relate to and discover and then be more refined versions of ourselves.

Our lifestyle changes our energy emanations and sets up a natural magnetic attractor pattern that allows us to increase our pranic flow by drawing us closer to the divine heat-cosmic fire of our Essence.

This cosmic fire is pure divine love and in this fire we are reborn, regenerated, made whole and complete and set free.

With cosmic fire as divine love as our dominant frequency pattern or harmonic, we enter easily into the Kingdom of Heaven energy flow of the highest dimensions within and around us.

So it is and so it always has been.

Key 3
Virtues, virtues, virtues!

Although we can live the recommended 8-point lifestyle in Key 2, it is our heart energy that determines the dimensions we enter - its purity and whether it carries the octaves of compassion, empathy, humility, patience, plus all the other virtues that the human heart is capable of embracing.

Many of these virtues we have gained in other timelines and so they are already within us, either dormant or dominant. Life today, as this embodiment we now have, continues to teach us more for every suffering we endure delivers the gift of a virtue.

Without compassion for ourselves and others, or without enough humility, certain inner plane doors to various dimensions will remain hidden to us as all inner plane doors can only be opened by frequency matching.

Asking our Essence the following will speed up our access of entry to inner plane heavenly Kingdoms, if this is possible.

"I ask now to joyously embody all the virtues required for me to enter into a lasting state of Divine Marriage with the Essence I AM. May these virtues be gained in the perfect way and time for me with joy and ease and Grace!"

Remember that all must unfold in its own way and time and some experiences in the gaining of virtues must be lived through fully in order for this virtue to become a deep and integral part of us.

Practical Exercise:-
- Take a few deep breaths, relax and then allow a word that represents a virtue, to come intuitively to you now.
- *Please note...* We want this word to be revealed from deep within you intuitively and not to come to you using your normal mental plane of thought and assessment after having understood why we are asking for this. This is an intuitive exercise.
- *So, be open, be still, what word is coming into your mind now that represents a virtue?*
- Next contemplate this word that you have received, then take a moment to meditate on what this virtue means to you in your life....
- *Now read on...*
- This virtue that you have just received the name of; is the virtue your Essence is guiding you now to focus more on in your life, as the deeper experience, or acceptance of this virtue is actually a personal Key for you to now to experience more of the gifts that your Essence has to share with you.
- Then use the *Breath Test* that we will soon share, to check how long your Essence would like you to focus on this virtue. A week, a month, a year?

- I once spent a year focussed totally on the virtue of *appreciation* and found that my happiness levels doubled even though I was already happy; I also found that all my relationships improved. In the exercise that my Essence gave me, I was to let go of all judgment and just be appreciative of everything that was unfolding in my life.

Key 4
Clarity, will and intention!

Having already experienced so much of this three dimensional duality-based world, many long to move on and in to a more peaceful realm while others hold the sincere desire to know who they truly are, to experience that they are more than just a physical system of mind and emotions. Still others are ready for a higher, more refined dimension of expression where peace and harmony are our natural rhythms; a dimension that many others have now glimpsed or enjoyed and now dwell in.

Most people in our world are interested in health, happiness and harmony. Hence, one clear intention we can hold is the following program of command which is designed to allow our complete bio-system to free itself of all human hungers and to do this in a harmonious way:

Program of Command – to be meditated on and then said with sincere hearted intention…

- "I love, honour and recognise my physical body intelligence. With respect, as the Essence I AM, I now give my physical body permission to feed itself in whatever way is for its highest good and health. Body; feed yourselves from cosmic micro food – as pranic Essence – or from physical food, or both, if required, now!"
- "I love honour and recognise the intelligence of my emotionally body energy system. With respect, as the Essence I AM, I give my emotional body permission to feed itself in whatever way required so that I attain emotional health and happiness now!"
- "I love honour and recognise my mental body intelligence. With respect, as the Essence I AM, I give my mental body permission to feed itself appropriately now!"

- *"The end result of this physical, emotional and mental body feeding is that I now exist in the rhythm of health, happiness and harmony within myself and with all life! So it is! So it is! So it is!"*

This pure clear command of intention will allow the bodies to move beyond their usual feeding patterns and to work together to bring our life rhythm into health, happiness and harmony which is the natural rhythm of our Essence imbued nature.

There are of course other programs of power that we have discussed throughout many of our research manuals and also in our "Liquid Universe – Advanced Bioshield Programming" (discourse-meditation) at this link:- http://www.jasmuheen.com/products-page/audio-books/liquid-universe-advanced-bioshield-programming-discourse-meditation/

Even the clear command of ...

"I AM LOVE, I AM INFINITE, I AM ETERNAL" that we use with the love breath meditation technique will also quickly align us to our pure Essence nature since these are the characteristics of the Christed Essence we carry within, where the word Christed just means a Being of pure love.

~7~
BEING ESSENCE

The benefits to our selves and our world in BEing Essence and identifying with our Essence nature much more than with our personality ego selves, is obvious. When this becomes a real experience through the use of the keys to Kingdom, rather than a nice sounding ideology, then our presence in any realm of existence becomes that of a giver rather than a hungry taker.

The true breatharian, in its purest form, is someone who has shifted their identification away from their limited personality self, to depending upon and entering into Sacred Marriage with the limitless divine resource of the Essence we carry within.

This Essence then regulates and controls our life, rather than allowing our more limited physical, emotional or mental body systems to be our boss in life.

For example with living physically from prana, our Essence then controls our weight when we surrender the body system to it, and we are freed via personal experience, from the idea that we need physical food to be healthy or to maintain the ideal weight.

As healers, artists and others open to the Divine Love flow of their own Essence, they are finding now that this Essence is physically feeding them and so they need to adjust and lessen their physical food intake in order not to gain unwanted weight.

Others all around the world are also now naturally eating less and lighter foods as they enter into deeper levels of experience and divine communion and oneness with their Essence.

Yet this too is just one small aspect of Being Essence.

In Being Essence we move from our thinking-and-doing-brains to the super-conscious-being-brain which provides us with huge creativity and the ability to access and download phenomenal levels of inter-dimensional data, for the Being Essence brain becomes that of the theta brain waved patterned child.

Jesus said at one point that in order to enter into the Kingdom of Heaven we must come as children. While we can interpret this in many ways, I like to look at this in terms of brain wave patterns.

Children aged 0-2 are known in general to be in a slower Delta brain wave pattern, similar to a long term meditator in deep meditation. From ages 2-6 they enter into the Theta brain wave pattern that also comes from the lifestyle we suggest in Key 2.

It is interesting to note that children from ages 0, or birth to 6, are in super-learning capacity absorbing and learning how to exist in life, to walk, feed, talk, learn languages and so much more.

Here in Theta frequency their brain is in super-plasticity with neural networks being born and reformed in ways that we no longer do when older. In this zone they have access to the world of their invisible friends and their levels of creativity and their imagination knows no bounds.

In this state they have a joyous innocence and simplicity that is so easy to love and be in the presence of. To them everything is fascinating and they tend to see endless fields of potential and possibility, at least until we as adults begin to condition them with our limited systems of control.

From age 6-12 their brain wave patterns move into Alpha and from age 12 the complete Beta-Alpha-Theta-Delta spectrum is available to us all.

Unfortunately our Western education system tends to stimulate predominantly left brain and Beta brain wave patterns which are reinforced by any toxic feeding, feeling and thinking patterns that we may still engage in.

Choosing to explore the other versions of ourselves by opening to experience the truth of the highest wisdoms of all the Holy Messengers that have expressed their Essence over time; also asking our Essence to rise and be the perfect guide and guru in our lives; plus opening and asking to experience all Its gifts, sets us once more on the path of intelligent, loving awareness where the Garden of Eden is easily found.

As above, so below.

We come as vast Beings, an extension of pure Essence from the Great Central Sun and to this state we can easily return.

It is just a matter of applying a few keys and shifting our identification for we are it all. We are humans with personalities vast and complex and yet quietly supporting this play of illusion in this world is a vast and loving field of wisdom with infinite power to create with care that which is for the highest good of all.

Creating from this point of awareness allows us to discover the Kingdom of Heaven that is within the All.

So it is and so it always has been.

Tread Lightly

Tread lightly through this world with grace,
tread lightly til your find your place,
tread lightly through these changing times
until your heart can find its rhyme.

Tread lightly til awareness grows,
of perfect paths, of things you know,
will bring you back to love again,
with its sweet doors to wisdom's plane.

Tread lightly til your joy it flows,
tread lightly til all seeds you sew,
can blossom in the light and sun
and bring you fruit from what's begun.

Tread sweetly on this path of love
until you wear compassion's glove.
Tread lightly on this earth right now
until it's time to take that bow.

For end times come of olden ways,
as prophecy proclaims new ways.
Until this game is played and done,
tread lightly and just be love's sun.

**OUR ESSENCE
as a
BASELINE FREQUENCY
plus
PRAGMATIC ALIGNMENTS**

While the previous pages hold more than
enough information to positively
transform all life,
we now offer some additional
KEYS TO THE KINGDOM
that many in our global seminars
have also experienced to be
practical and beneficial in life!

Our Baseline Essence

- In interdimensional energy field science, a BASELINE is a frequency that directs and supports the flow of events in creation.
- As an energy pulse, a baseline also determines our experiences in life.
- The real baseline frequency in every one of us is what many call ESSENCE.
- Others call our baseline the presence of God, chi or an energy force that is within all life.
- In the human energy pool, our baseline Essence (B.E.) can be strong or weak depending on our utilisation of it.
- The more we utilise our B.E. (Baseline Essence) the freer and easier existence becomes for ourselves and our planet.
- Other benefits from the utilisation of our B.E. are increased health, happiness and harmony levels.
- A stronger experience of our baseline Essence also increases feelings of well-being and deep peace.
- The B.E. in all is limitless, pure, perfect and complete – always there, always available.
- Able to provide for us all in the most unexpected ways, our B.E. is the most significant free resource we all have at our disposal.
- Access to this baseline Essence is easy and we can all tune to it and feel it via our breath as it is the force that breathes us.
- Awareness of our B.E. can begin the most amazing journey as we open to discover its gifts and attributes.
- Because of the type of frequency our baseline Essence is, merging consciously back into its pure energy pool is completely transformational.
- To do this collectively will revolutionise our world, because our B.E. is so powerful as it has brought all creation into Being.
- Not only is our baseline Essence powerful, it also carries within itself the wisdom and the way to resolve all of the imbalances in our world.
- The power and wisdom of our B.E. is enhanced further by the harmonic pulse of a LOVE that can eliminate all our emotional, mental and spiritual hunger.
- Reunification with our B.E. energy current allows a body freedom from many basic human needs.

- Able to love, guide, heal and also physically feed us, the more we utilise our baseline Essence as a nourishment source, the less dependant we are on earth based resources.
- A strong B.E. can also free the human bio-system of all dis-ease, which will in turn free planet Earth from all disease.

The exact "How to's" of making the Presence of our Baseline Essence stronger, plus how to utilise this energy even more effectively in our lives, will be covered next.

OUR PARADISE

Codes & Meditations

We offer the additional Keys to the Kingdom to take us beyond any religious separation and so unify our various realities more into the One People living in harmony on One Planet agenda of the Embassy of Peace.

The following basic but clear Meditations and Codes also have the power to transform and redirect human evolution when they are applied with sincerity and the understanding of how our thoughts and our feelings create our reality.

1. Law of Love plus Meditation
2. Prayer Power, Prayer Time
3. Peace & Paradise Codes
4. Perfect Communication - Essence to Essence
5. Three Level Guidance System
6. Breath Test Guidance plus meditation
7. B.E. - Baseline Essence Meditation

The Law of Love
(as discussed in our book *The Law of Love*)

The Law of Love states that all life, all atoms, all molecules, all energy fields have come into existence due to the love of the original force of creation. It also states that when we treat all life with love, honour and respect, as if it is a part of us, then the law of love will magnetise us to its river of grace and embrace us back into itself as one of its own.

The Law of Love also states that divine love, as the original force of creation, has the power to transmute everything it touches back into its original form.

The Law of Love finds the seekers of miracles and its grace teaches us how to recognise, enjoy and also how to create them, and in the experiencing of these miracles we find ourselves already made perfect and also free.

Miracles are said to be wonders performed by super-natural powers, a sign or an expression of a special gift. Coming from the Latin word 'miracula' the witnessing of miracles often promotes awe, or excitement, for such an act is seen to come from Divine Grace. Grace is a sign that we are aligned to the Law of Love in life and with our Essence nature.

Meditation:-
- As you sit and still yourself in meditation, you might like to align to this pure rhythm of divine love that is deep within us all.
- Just slowing the breathing rhythm right down, holding an intention that you are open to experiencing this pure love pulse that is within you now,
- and as you meditate on this infinite flow of pure loving energy that has given birth to creation, you might like to keep your mind focused on the chant 'I AM LOVE' ...
- chant this slowly on the inhale, 'I ... AM ... LOVE'
- and on the exhale imagine radiating pure love out through every pore of your skin and then out into the world to share this pure Essence with others as you slowly chant 'I ... LOVE'.

The chant 'I AM LOVE' and 'I LOVE' aligns our vibration into the energy field of the Essence that has brought the Law of Love to life.

- Continue to take deep … slow … refined … gentle breaths …
- open with each breath to feel the purest, deepest rhythms of love within the very matrix of creation
- sense how these rhythms are pulsing deep within you now …
- play with your breathing rhythm until you feel the pulse of love that your Essence has for you …

Prayer Power, Prayer Time
(as discussed in our book *Four Body Fitness: Biofields & Bliss*)

Prayer can also be called Divine Communion, it is a way to connect with the Universal Field of Infinite Love and Intelligence that we know flows throughout creation as a baseline Essence. One of the most honouring things we can do in acknowledgement this Baseline Essence that some also call God, is to talk from our heart of hearts with this force of intelligence as if it is our best friend.

The Bulgarian sage Omraam Mikhaël Aïvanhov said on prayer, "*I much prefer a prayer that is unrehearsed, one that flows spontaneously. When you ask a favour of a friend, you speak simply and naturally, without affectation.*" It is suggested that this is how we should pray, unscripted and with a sincere heart.

A 1988 Duke University study team proved the power of prayer as a healing tool when they asked people from many different religious groups to pray for patients who had undergone massive cardiac procedures. While the group didn't know they were being prayed for, at the end of this study they found that patients were between 50-100% better when someone prayed for them in comparison to other patients for whom no special prayers were said. All the various religious groups participating achieved the same results.

Brief Meditation and Prayer time ...

- Let us get comfortable and then close our eyes to ready ourselves to take a few moments in prayer Firstly, ...
- slow your breathing rhythm right down and open to be aware of your Baseline Essence deep within, the supreme force of intelligence that is always listening and always there.
- Sense via your breath and by expanding your awareness of It, that It is a flow of wisdom that exists throughout all of creation, that It supports us through life via our breath ...
- Imaging this force is always aware of us as Its creation ...
- What do you need to share from your deepest heart to this Essence now?

- Just slow your breathing rhythm down even further, making it more subtle and refined so that you can feel the presence of your Essence and hear Its voice of higher knowing …
- breathing slow, deep, gentle, refined breaths …
- Exactly what do you need to share from your deepest heart with this pure Essence now?
- Imagine It alert within you and listening …
- Perhaps you pray for peace in our world … or the light of love and wise understanding …
- Perhaps you pray for someone in need …
- or instead, perhaps you use this prayer time to give gratitude for all the wonder in your own life and for the beauty of creation.

A simple prayer:-

"Essence of Creation, within me and around me and in all life …
I ask now to be tuned more deeply to your channel of infinite love and wisdom, with joy and ease and Grace.
I ask also for the clarity and wisdom, the higher vision to always walk a path in this life that is for my highest good and the highest good of all.
I ask for the all the support that I require here now to joyously fulfil all that I have come to do in this life in harmony with all. So it is! So it is! So it is!"

Another simple prayer:-

"Thank you, thank you, thank you! I give this prayer of gratitude now for all the wonderful people, things and experiences that continue to fill and bless my life! I feel truly blessed for …
(then list all the things that you feel truly grateful for in your life today …)"

Peace and Paradise Codes
(as discussed in our book *Four Body Fitness: Biofields & Bliss*)

The quantum field is programmed naturally to respond to each human energy system as if we are all powerful, creative and intrinsically divine beings. Hence it responds to our dominant thought, word and emotion patterns and reflects these back to us in every moment as our reality.

Research done by American bio-chemist Dr Bruce Lipton on human DNA, has also found that our DNA can be altered by our perception and environment.

According to researchers this means we are not hardwired and proves the higher light science premise that we can easily rewire, not just our brains neural pathways but also our genetic pre-disposition and also change and reset our DNA.

This supports the idea that we can work with our Essence, the Divine One Within us, to continually repattern and remodel our selves into the best versions of our selves that we can manifest.

Inter-dimensional biofield science asserts that we are almost like robots who are continually responding to our own self created DNA signals. Nonetheless our ability to exist with a body in physical matter is part of the Divine DNA Code; a code that is held in our Baseline Essence.

Therefore, a code command that we can use to realign our current DNA back to our Divine DNA flow is:

"I ask to realign all my human DNA patterning back to my original, perfect, Divine DNA NOW! I ask the intelligent universal flows within and around me, this Baseline Essence, to align every energy flow within and around me NOW in to the energy field of peace ... paradise ... health ... happiness ... and harmony ... NOW!"

Just meditate on the above code further then say it again with a sincere heart, feeling as if it is your right as a Divine Being in form to once again experience personal and global paradise and peace.

The below Code is also beneficial in our conscious realignment into the Paradise realms that already exist as a subtle dimension in this world.

"Divine DNA Paradise Grid lock-in Now! Divine DNA Paradise Grid lock-in NOW! Divine DNA ... Paradise Grid ... lock-in ... NOW! ... I claim my birthright as a human being on Earth, to exist in the rhythm of peace, to know this world as a paradise place again NOW! So it is! So it is! So it is!"

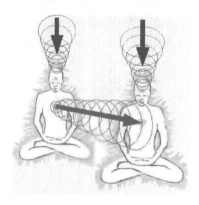

Perfect Communication Essence to Essence
The DOW Match Code
(as discussed in our book *Four Body Fitness: Biofields & Bliss*)

Like many I am interested in higher levels of communication that take us beyond ego, past timeline influences plus educational and cultural differences which we can do by communicating directly with each other, Essence to Essence.

Our DOW is the Divine One Within us all – our Essence. The DOW Match Code has the potential if sincerely said and intended by enough people, to facilitate perfect communication and harmonize and empower us all.

Chanting *"DOW Match now!"*, or *"Divine Communion Now!"* or even *"Essence Connection Now!"* silently with sincerity 3 times when we meet someone is a wonderful way to harmonize our world and ourselves. Of course we can also just hold the clear intention that this *"Essence Connection"* happens automatically with everyone we meet from this moment on.

The DOW Match or *"Essence Connection"* command can be used with family, friends, colleagues and strangers after first extending our welcome to them. Sending a pink beam of love from your heart into theirs immediately you meet, changes the energy field resonance between you and opens you both to a purer form of energy communication.

Next imagine love of the highest order flowing between you as you look at them and silently say, *'Yes, I really do wish to have the most perfect relationship I can with this person and so I now ask for a DOW Match; to match frequencies Essence to Essence with everyone that I meet so that we can enjoy mutually beneficial relationships.'*

To DOW Match is an act of honour and respect and surrender. It's about stepping aside from our personal agendas and asking the Supreme Consciousness, our Essence to communicate through both parties.

This DOW Match command is about allowing the relationship to begin, if it is with a new person, or to continue with friends, to blossom into the most perfect exchange between you thus creating a WIN, WIN, WIN relationship – a win for you, a win for others and a win for the global energy field.

Asking for the DOW Match, or Essence Match, is the most selflessly loving thing that we can do for ourselves and others as it gives our Baseline Essence the opportunity to communicate with all, with everyone's pure Essence.

Brief Meditation:-

- Imagine all beings around you now on the inner plane ... standing in circles around you now ...
- Imagine your heart opens and a beam of pure pink light love flows out from your heart to connect with all around you now ...
- Imagine their heart is receiving this flow and opening and absorbing your love as well so all that is passing between you now is pure Essence as a Divine love flow ...
- and then we say with feeling - *"Baseline Essence connection, communication lock-in NOW! From this moment on with all beings I share pure Essence to pure Essence so that all unfolds now for the highest good of all in mutually enhancing and supportive ways!"*
- Meditate on this in silence for a few minutes.
- In this state of meditation you may also add a more specific code of intention, such as:-

"I ask my DOW, the Divine One Within me, my Essence, to now match to the Divine One Within with all my family, loved ones, friends and colleagues. I ask my DOW, my Essence, to match me Essence to Essence with all beings in the world who are open to connect in this way beyond external influences, culture and more! Connect us now, Essence to Essence with all, so that all our sharing is now unfolding for the highest good of all."

- Next we take a moment in this meditative state, to give thanks for all the people we have loved, who have loved us as well and for all people in our life that we love still.
- Focus also on the idea that all will now unfold between yourself, and all who you connect with, in a way that is for the highest good of all.

Baseline Essence Guidance
A 3 level confirmation system
(as discussed in our book *The Law of Love*)

The first level we have for gaining information that is beneficial for us is by connecting with, learning to tune to and hear our inner voice, the voice of our Baseline Essence, the Divine One Within all. This must always be our first method of testing in that it is the only reliable source of confirmation that is completely incorruptible. This requires us to establish a clear line of communication between ourselves and our Divine nature, whether we call this our DOW, Monad, Atman, I Am Presence, or Baseline Essence or just our Essence.

This level of communication comes via our 6th and 7th senses of intuition and knowing and I think that it needs to be our first barometer of guidance in everything that we do in life, particularly in accessing and manifesting our pre-agreement.

Our DOW – the Divine One Within us as Essence, is the only thing that all humanity has in common, It is pure, It gives us life, It breathes us, loves us and guides us to evolve into our perfection, to manifest the divinity we are in harmony with all. Learning to listen to It and trust its guidance is a basic part of self-mastery and self-knowledge.

The second level of testing is to use the art of kinesiology to gain information, confirmation, using muscle responses in the body. Kinesiology, as many trained in this skill know, has its limitations because it depends on how it is used, how strongly people's muscles test, and it also depends on the calibration purity of the one being tested, the one doing the testing and the questions being asked.

Reading David Hawkins' book *Power vs. Force* will provide a deeper understanding on this subject. I also recommend that when we use kinesiology that we ask the Divine One Within, our Essence, to confirm data using the muscle testing system through the body rather than asking the physical body's consciousness itself as its focus is solely on survival, while the Essence is the all knowing wiser part of ourselves.

The third level of testing that is a wonderful support system for us as we journey through these changing and sometimes chaotic times, is to ask to receive clear confirmation from the Universal Field of Intelligence, which is within us as our Baseline Essence and all around us.

For example I remember once being very curious about information and going into a bookshop, where a book fell off the top shelf, hit me on the head, spiralled around and turned the right way up, open at my feet. When I picked this book up I found that on that open page was the exact answer to the question I had been thinking about for some time.

The Universal Field of Intelligence, as a flow of pure Essence, responds to our telepathic thought patterns when we have a strong desire for further knowledge, particularly when the knowledge we are seeking is supporting our own evolutionary path in a positive way that is also beneficial for this world.

Yet my favourite technique of all is number one, using that inner Essence, the Baseline Essence with Its flows of wisdom to confirm the answer to any questions we may have.

Apart from trusting our initial intuitive reactions, there is a simple method we can use to do this, for this Baseline Essence breathes us and when we make a statement that is not in alignment with Its' will, then It will change the way that It breathes through us.

We call this method of testing the *Breath Test*.

Remember we live in a time now of great chaos and change, it is a time of self-reliance, self-responsibility and learning to trust and listen to that divine voice of infinite wisdom and love within.

So let's practice this breath test now ...

Baseline Essence Guidance System - Breath Test

- Just think for a moment about something simple that you know is a complete lie for you, something simple like, "My body really loves meat" for example, which for a vegetarian is not true.
- As you chant this over and over as if it is a truth, just watch what your breath does …
- breathe normally as you watch what is happening in your body as you keep chanting this lie over and over as if it is a truth.

- Now take a moment to think of something that you know to be absolutely 100% true for you, something simple, like perhaps the statement, "*I really love my family*" or find something else to chant that is absolutely true for you
- then begin to chant this simple truth over and over as a statement of fact while again you watch what your normal breath does
- be very aware that there is an energy force breathing you and how it is reacting to this chant …
- Take a moment to practise this before you read on.

Results or signs:- Many people find that when they make a statement that is true for them, that is 100% in alignment with the will of the Essence that is breathing them, that physically it feels as if the breath drops right down to the stomach, or to the intestinal area, and that the organs, especially the lungs, seem to expand or open up.

They also find that when they make a statement that is not a truth for their Essence, then the Essence that is breathing them lets them know by allowing the breath to rise up towards the nose or else it seems to get stuck in the throat, often with the feeling as if everything, including the lungs, is closing down or contracting inside. Others can also notice a change in the beat of their heart or sense other signs in the physical body that are a clear physical response as directed by their Essence, to a statement they are making.

Just play with this rhythm for a while, thinking of something that you may not be sure about in your life that you would like confirmation for, always make it as a statement as if it's true for you, whether you know that it is or not, and then watch what your breath does.

I like to always start this breath test with ...
"It is beneficial for me to … (insert the statement)."
Or
"It is for my highest good to… (insert the statement.)"
Or
"It is for my highest good, and the highest good of my work in this world, to … (insert the statement.)"

While many long term meditators are great at receiving clear inner guidance, sometimes tuning ourselves into true stillness, to be able to hear our inner voice, can take time.

This breath test technique is a quick and simple way for us to receive inner guidance from our Essence wherever we are and whenever we need quick confirmation without having to go into deep meditation. It also means we never have to give our power away to anyone again, as through this simple technique we can always know what is true for us.

If there is no response when you are well practiced at receiving results from this technique, it may simply be that regarding this information you are seeking confirmation on, that it is not your time to know the answer yet, or that what you are seeking to know is none of your business.

However this technique tends to work very well when we check information for others and when we seek data that is for their highest good as well, for our Essence is their Essence and it is all knowing, all loving, all wise, existing everywhere and breathing through us all in every moment.

So practice this technique until it becomes a quick response mechanism for you, where you find that you can simply make a statement once or twice in your head telepathically to Essence within and see how the breath responds … breathing always naturally … always making a statement as if it is true.

This technique can be used before making any important, potentially life changing decision.

BEing Essence Meditation

- We take a few moments of deep … slow … gentle breathing …
- imagine with each slow, deep inhale that we are drawing from deep within us, an endless stream of pure Essence energy …
- and on the exhale we just relax, breathing out slowly, letting go of everything but our focus on this pure internal energy pool, our Essence …
- Slow … deep … inhale,
- drawing this Essence up from the very core of our Being,
- relaxing deeper into this Essence on each exhale
- Slowing the breathing rhythm down further with the intention to connect more deeply with the one that is breathing us … our Essence …
- with each slow inhale … imagine it rising gently, strengthening within …
- with each slow exhale let go of everything but this moment of opening to feel pure Essence rise with each slow, deep yet refined inhale …

- Imagining this Essence as pure and perfect, that enlightened part of you already healed and whole, this is the internal energy pool that you are now drawing from with each slow inhale,
- then, relaxing on the exhale, let go back into the pure Essence energy pool, all that concerns you or is taking you away from this moment.
- Perhaps this pure Essence is another part of yourself that you know so well through your meditations … or perhaps this part of you has not yet been met,
- and so we relax and open to its flow,
- drawing it up from our deep inner core, to flood our bodies with each slow inhale …
- Sense It as a loving, wise, powerful being, your inner Guru, your own wise One within …
- Imagine mixing and blending all of your energies with this pure Essence as It rises within you,
- with each slow, inhale, imagine Its energy is now rising within you to present Its love to you, like a parent embracing a long lost child, or greeting a well loved friend …
- Taking deep … slow … connected breaths,
- as your exhale flows gently to the inhale, hold the intention that you are drawing in energy from the highest dimensions within you,
- that you are drawing up to be more fully present within you, your pure Essence energy which can and now is able to nourish you on all levels of your Being …
- Imagine as It rises, that It is transforming you, recalibrating you, imbuing you with Its pure Self…
- perhaps you sense It as a cooling fire that rises and burns off all within you, all that no longer serves you, allowing you to feel reborn with every breath,
- then with each exhale we let go, relax your whole body and sense as if you are now sinking deeper into this pure and perfect ascended pool of energy that we all carry deep within …
- take deeper, slower breaths as you imagine you are drinking of this infinitely wise, loving Essence within …
- imagine your Essence filling your cellular structure, then exhale and let It then flow out through the pores of our skin into this world to nourish everything around that is open to this flow of pure Essence …

- Slowly deep inhale and then relax deeper into your Essence on each exhale.
- With each deep, slow breath always imagine that you are drinking of this infinitely wise, loving Essence within …
- enjoying the silence as you keep your mind focused on drawing this pure Essence up from the very core of your true being, letting It rise …
- allowing It to do what It needs to do as It floods through your system, feeding you emotionally, mentally, spiritually, physically …
- Imagining Its flow adjusting you now, back into the rhythm of health, happiness, harmony …
- Sense and know with each slow breath, that we are pure, wise, loving Beings as we let this Essence rise and radiate through our life …
- The mantra that we often use with this breath technique is "I AM".
- On the slow inhale we slowly chant "I", identifying with the Supreme, Divine I within
- And on the exhale we slowly chant "AM".
- The "I AM" mantra is one of the oldest in our world that acknowledges the Supreme "*I AM THAT I AM*" in all.
- Take a few moments now with this breathing rhythm and intention and add the mantra I AM.
- Be aware of any changes in your body with this.

Do this breath technique morning and night for at least 5 – 10 minutes to begin and end each day feeling more aware of your Essence.

Being HEALTHY

- Our rhythm of health is determined by how we spend out time.
- Awareness of what can be, plus smart choices, help enormously in finding a healthy rhythm.
- Health, happiness and harmony can be ours with the right attitudes and lifestyle.
- As many now know, our health of body is also directly related to the health of our spirits, hearts and minds.
- Health is also about moving through life in harmony, adding to the whole in a positive way as well as we can; this means being aware of others; choosing to interact in a mutually enhancing - M.E. - way.
- The M.E. manner is about holding clear intent and acting in ways that add to the whole positively, i.e. enhancing all, being enhanced by all.
- Another Code for this may be:

"All my relationships with all life, operate in a mutually beneficial manner! I ask that this be manifested now as truth!"

- To achieve energy fields that are mutually enhancing means Self responsibility, self nurturing and calling all of our behaviours into better rhythms that add health to the whole, to ourselves and what we are creating.
- We do this via lifestyle choice.
- A healthy heart is a persona that cares for the welfare of all.
- Healthy hearts give and receive love freely and easily, supported in life by the flow of Grace.
- A healthy mind is one that is open to the best solution for all, which we can arrive at by using the Triple Win Code.

You may wish to state with feeling:

"I ask for perfect resolution to all areas of personal and global conflict; resolutions that deliver a win for me, a win for others and a win for this world! I ask that these be downloaded into the hearts and minds of all those involved for perfect resolution Triple Win now!"

- Healthy spirits love to help if required, to shine a light to positive paths that serve us all. This also means caring about our planet as if she truly is beloved and using her resources with efficiency and wisdom for support.

Code: *"I love, honour and respect our planet and live well in Gaia's world"*. We take from her, we give back even more.

- What is the most effective way to giveback to the spirit of our world, Gaia?
- Perhaps we can personally consume less resources?
- To do this, we can experience and then depend upon, our B.E. Prana Resource Pool.
- A healthy person's Baseline Essence is always present and flowing within them. Its pulse can therefore nourish all aspects of itself, including Its physical body 'house'.
- A healthy mind/body connection, allows us to know the body as a microcosm of atoms and cells held together by Essence as a glue, that can be felt as love.
- A healthy heart can sing us through life, filling us with peace and the wonderment of creation.
- A healthy heart-mind sees and knows the bigger picture, and guides as required or asked. It knows the benefit of operating in mutually enhancing ways.
- Health comes via our commitment to conduct our lives via a specific operating system that achieves this.
- Again, the best system we have found at the Embassy of Peace is the 8 point Luscious Lifestyles Program - L.L.P. as discussed previously and in our YouTube videos.
- This lifestyle is designed to bring us into health, happiness and harmony on personal, emotional, mental and spiritual levels. It is free and easily accessible by all.

You may also enjoy the Code:
"I am the rhythm of health, happiness and harmony. I open to experience and enjoy this rhythm NOW!"

There is more to the rhythm of health of course yet this is a simple start. Keep it simple – do what feels right in your heart of hearts.

OUR ESSENCE
AS A SOURCE OF COSMIC MICRO-FOOD

As we move into a higher dimension of expression, which is a result of BEing more imbued with our Essence, we find that It can also provide us with a type of physical body nourishment that I have come to call *Cosmic Micro-food*.

Due to the beneficial effects that our research has found, that this can have on both our health and our environment, we will include some of the basics of this here on a bigger picture level.

To me, one of the most fulfilling journeys a soul can make while anchored in the plane of duality, is awareness of and full reconnection and perfect union with their I AM Essence.

Yet unity consciousness allows us to feel-sense that Essence as being everywhere, the very fabric of creation, the baseline frequency of life.

Apart from being able to nourish us physically via its cosmic micro-food flow, it also aligns us to a rhythm of such peace and contentment, that we find ourselves forever transformed.

Its gifts are endless.

Its ability to love, guide, heal and nourish us completely, is natural yet profound. It reveals itself in Its own way, in Its own time, when the energy streams can match It within us and around us, and yet we are never separate from It, It is always there, just Its volume alters, the strength or subtlety with which It flows.

All of this we can control by understanding the science of pranic living, which is the science of being Essence.

While we have already written five books on the being-physically-nourished-by-prana reality which share much more detail about this; the key to being able to be free from the need to take physical food and fluid, is to be anchored in the versions of ourselves that are most imbued with Essence.

This makes the Breatharian reality a spiritual journey and not a diet, for this intake of cosmic micro food comes from direct access to our Essence and its multi-dimensional nature.

Everyone has a version of themselves that has this freedom. We all have multi-dimensional, inter-dimensional versions that are already the true

Breatharian, versions that exist without form as a flow of intelligent loving consciousness.

We all have versions of ourselves that are also so light-filled yet still in form, that prana as Essence, is the natural source of nourishment.

It is impossible to live without physical food or fluid intake if all we focus on is our personality self with its Beta brain function living in a dual natured world.

Yet a breatharian is said to be a breather of God and God as Essence breathes us all. As we shift identification to our Essence nature, feel It, experience all Its gifts including the choice of where we wish to take our physical body nourishment from, then we find that not only is our Essence as a God-like force, breathing us, but that we are in Essence the pure I AM that some call God.

Our Baseline Essence
Resource of Nourishment (Living on Light)

- Our Essence is our life force which is pure prana.
- To understand how we can utilise our Baseline Essence (B.E.) as an internal resource, we need to understand its composition, i.e. what our B.E. contains.
- As an energy source, our B.E. holds all the building blocks of life and all creation has the same baseline Essence woven through it.
- For example, a cotton shirt cannot be made until the cotton has been sown as seeds, then grown, harvested and woven, and from this fabric many types of garments can be made. Our baseline is like the cloth, a weave that runs through all.
- Similarly the fabric of creation can be woven in many different ways. Some is woven into universes, galaxies, solar system, planets, human and other life forms.
- How the B.E. expresses Itself, and Its very existence in everything, then becomes the common denominator of all as It is in all.
- As the supporting fabric of creation, our Baseline Essence has every vitamin, mineral, element, chemical, electro-magnetic pulse potential and much more than a human body could need to utilise.

- Therefore feeding our body and living purely on prana – or our Baseline Essence - is not about *creating* an alternate source of nourishment.
- Instead we just need to tap into what is *already* in our Baseline Essence, and allow it to do what it has always known how to do even though we have forgotten this.
- Merging our awareness and aligning our bio-system back with our B.E. brings many additional gifts apart from our Its ability to physically nourish us.
- We tap into our B.E. in many different ways, yet the process begins by our acknowledgement of our B.E. as an internal resource that we all can access.
- Acknowledgement of our B.E. is easier also when it is not just an idea but a tangible experience.
- Experiencing our B.E. comes from matching frequencies with it, which we do via the Luscious Lifestyle Program that also emphasises Baseline Essence identification and conscious alignment.
- *Due to the Universal Law of Resonance, our B.E. also grows via our focus upon it.*
- Our B.E. contains a field of infinite intelligence. In this field is the innate knowing of how to keep a life-form alive and healthy on all levels.
- In fact, our B.E. holds pre-programmed data flows on how to access anything we need to be self-sustaining and feel whole and complete.
- Thus it is the perfect teacher.
- Our steps then so far are:- attitudes of acknowledgement, allowance, and lifestyle alignment on a day to day basis.
- Allowance requires a mindset shift, holding the awareness that we only eat for pleasure not for need as we know our Baseline Essence can feed us.
- While food is wonderful to consume, it is nice to know we do not need it and to have a greater choice in how we wish to be nourished.
- Next we need to lovingly invite our physical body system to open to receive a perfect blend of nourishment from all healthy sources including Cosmic Micro-food (or Chi, as prana) which is also our Baseline Essence.
- We can also lovingly instruct our complete bio-system to open to our Essence as a source of perfect nutrition.
- We can intend this to occur within our physical, emotional, mental and spiritual systems.

- We can further ask our intelligent B.E. for us to be so well nourished on all levels, that we exist with Grace and ease in the rhythm of health, happiness, harmony and mutual enhancement with all.
- This program of intention allows us to be a self-sustaining mechanism on all levels not just physically.
- Next we need to learn to talk to and listen to the physical body. Stop eating out of habit. Eat only when and if you are hungry while you hold firm in the knowledge of what your B.E. can do for you.
- Begin to eat less and eat more live and light foods. Go from 3 meals per day to 2 then 2 meals a day to 1. Put less on your plate – eat only until you are no longer hungry and not until you are full, as research has shown that this is better for you.
- Via meditation, tune to your body consciousness and ask it what it wants you to eat, rather than what you think it needs.
- Learn the B.E. Guidance breath test technique that we have already shared and use it to check your prana percentage on a regular basis and improve this percentage via your lifestyle.
- Using this method make the statement ...

  "Prana now provides more than 50% of my physical body nourishment!"

  If the breath confirms this, then check using the same statement for more than 60% and so on until you ascertain your exact prana percentage.

  Anytime you get a no response with the breath test, then drop the percentage amount you are checking, down as maybe your prana % is 40%, or even 49% for example.

  If you get a yes to 50% then you can safely reduce your physical food intake by that % amount.

  However if you do this, you must also hold the intention that:

  "All my vitamins, all my minerals and everything I need to be a healthy, self regenerating, self sustaining system comes directly to me from prana as my Essence."
- Full conversion to living purely on prana and our B.E. cannot be attempted until this level reads 100% and your complete bio-system is hooked in.
- Note: while your mental and physical systems can often handle a quick conversion, the emotional body system can take much longer.
- Conversion rates vary within our own bio-system, as well as person to person, as each is unique.

- The embodiment of certain virtues is also important as a mode of accessing a stronger flow of Essence energy to the degree that a pure, pranic flow can feed us.
- Use the B.E. Guidance System to assess your required virtue components for an easy transition. Which ones need more attention and development?
- With sincere hearted intention, ask your Baseline Essence to guide you into this experience of nourishment organically, in the rhythm of joy, ease and Grace, in the right way and time for you.
- Know and trust that your B.E. is your perfect energy resource of love, wisdom and true nourishment, by using meditation to experience what your Essence really is!
- Be more conscious of the Divine Resource within and use It to free you from, or lessen, your dependence on the world's food resources.

TREAT YOUR BODY WITH LOVE AND CARE.
For a more detailed guidance system on this please read
"The Food of Gods" & also "The Prana Program"

The versions of ME ...

I love the versions of me that are well connected, hard wired into my Essence. These versions are healthy, happy and content; they are older wiser versions of me that are also still evolving in so many different ways. All my aspects - my artist self (who loves to put color into form on canvas), my musical self (who feels like such a novice, someone open now to reclaim the mastery of tones), the version of me as an Ambassador of peace, the mother and grandmother me, the funny bohemian me plus many more, and even the version of me who is erroneously said by some to be the leader of the global breatharian movement ... all of my versions coalesce continually to form the movie of my life with each one playing different parts.

There are so many layers of ourselves and so many subtle realms for us all to explore. Tuning through it all, dancing as best we can through life, we eventually realize there really is nothing for us to do except to relax down deep through all these the levels, until we find the versions of ourselves that are most imbued with our Essence for it is here that we find true contentment in this human existence. And the best news is that there are simple pathways to being more powerfully imbued with our Essence, that part of us that exists in this inner kingdom of ours. And so we can relax knowing these versions also exist already pure and perfect within us, so all we need to do is tune deeper into them and then enjoy the version of our choice!

And so I slide my focus, to levels deep within,
to sit in contemplation and feel its glow, its skin.

Yes, I AM pure ESSENCE, that exists as love in all.
We are just rising Essence, a flow, at wisdom's ball.

I AM flowing through the Matrix, as a golden pulse of light,
I am swimming in wide rivers now carried by love's tide.

Essence Networks
"The Tribe of I AM"

Knowing, sensing, BEing Essence and existing in unity consciousness can connect us into the most amazing metaphysical network of compassionate and aware people.

While each individual is unique, each person is an extension of our own 'I AM-Essence' who is choosing to express itself with a certain outcome in mind. Therefore everyone's energy rhythms - like mine - will be, are being and have been, regularly altered and refined as we all grow and learn in this dense three dimensional world.

Yet each I AM extension, and hence every life-form fits in perfectly to the tapestry of life, with everyone adding something to the greater pool. All the suffering and the pain eventually brings wisdom and joy again when we see it all from an expanded view or just in retrospection. From knowing all of this, from seeing and feeling it this way, we become more relaxed and free.

I give and receive energetically in a mutually enhancing rhythm as this makes the most sense to me. I study, sense and play with the rhythms of life so that I can be more imbued with pure Essence, whose natural network I call the tribe of the I AM.

The I AM tribe are people who are focussed on Being Essence and they are every where. On our planet alone the I AM Essence is exploring being in 7 billion bodies an dis also exploring being all forms of mineral, plant and animal life and more.

Existence is filled with members of the I AM Tribe with some feeling absolute unity, joy and Oneness; while others are operating as completely separate energy streams, often feeling as if all they are is a mind, body and emotion system.

Saying yes to living true unity consciousness is like saying yes to the most perfect life experience that takes us way beyond the accepted day to day realities that many exist in.

To surround ourselves with the perfect life paradigm that enhances all, to say yes *"I live the perfect life that enhances us all!"* and mean it so that the I AM Essence we carry can support and deliver this as a truth, is also very freeing.

To say yes, to the heartfelt code:- *"I am the rhythm of health, happiness and harmony"* opens us up to these energy fields and magnetises this reality to us and us to it, as this is what heartfelt programs of clarity do.

To say yes to perfect resolution to all the conflict in life is also so freeing as we see all conflict dissolve when the Triple Win solutions kick in. As we have previously mentioned, to ask: *"Perfect Triple Win Resolution to all conflict that exists in my life and in this world now!"* is another great clear intention that when said sincerely frees us from duality and conflict.

Through the I AM Essence Tribe, we, as extensions of our own I AM, get to simultaneously experience all of creation and so be more aware and made bigger, brighter and smarter because of it all.

Somewhere there is a me, in this sea of we, who truly is a brilliant doctor, scientist, artist, musician, mime, sailor, sculptor, engineer, UFO pilot, ET, angel, ascended master and of course much more. All of us are aspects of the true us as we are all connected on the innernet by our Essence.

Knowing this, there is then nothing for us to chase or judge. There is also nothing for us to complain about as somewhere, if not here yet, we are living the perfect life and loving the life we are living. Or maybe not, as maybe somewhere else we are truly locked into suffering or struggle. Yet it all counts. It all has value as it all informs, and adds to, the whole.

And if our life isn't quite as we would like it to be we can easily change our personal rhythms and experience in life, by lovingly accepting the humanness of our personality self and then by choosing to identify more with our Essence by applying what we have suggested.

So right here, right now, I am the most relaxed I have ever been in my own life, for there is nothing to judge about myself or anyone else. Instead I can relax and enjoy life knowing that my own I AM Essence nature is exactly where it needs to be, that as my I AM Essence, I am exactly where I need to be.

Right here, right now, there is brilliant music to fill my heart and home, there's family to appreciate, enjoy and love.

Right here, right now, there is a big blue planet that I can walk upon, whose natural rhythms I feel everyday as the powerful being we call Gaia, a Cosmic Being who is currently undergoing great change.

There are also strangers who I have yet to meet who may soon be friends and there are friends who I can enjoy before they too eventually pass out of this known existence.

There are also many things yet to witness, other things yet to enjoy and create, plus the general game of life with so many rhythms to share, and so for me it truly is a joy to be in human form here now.

Today I felt the spring breeze spiralling up the valley to refresh me with its pranic flow; today I heard birds singing, felt the sun shining, and later listened to some heart-felt music from my iPod dock.

Today I felt as if it was indeed a perfect day and in this moment here now, a perfect life.

Could it be this simple, this shift to a higher octave of life, where we can all just BE our Essence and experience a time of pleasure and mutual gain?

Why not?

Allowance is freeing. To step back, let go and allow all of our I AM Essence extensions to just be as a tribe, to trust that all people are being guided by the same Essence, that each of us hold an awareness and thirst to explore life or rest now in life, depending on each persons' blueprint for this life.

As pure Essence Beings, we know that there is no death, so none can die, that instead each just changes form and that we age then die in accordance to our beliefs and how we choose to spend our time. This too is so freeing.

Knowing all of this, then our choices must be clear and we all need to be very conscious of what we wish to create as our creations continually affect the whole.

Living the type of lifestyle we have prescribed in much of our research work and also in the chapter "Keys to the Kingdom", frees us even more as disease and ill health are generally no more.

A strong spirit, body, mind connection plus well chosen thoughts and emotions that can nurture us all, these are also freeing, bringing peace to a life well lived via a future well thought out and a new moment to be just enjoyed.

So it is and so it always has been.

I Smile

I smile for the friends who have stood by me.
I smile for the light in all that I see.
I smile for the Grace that fills up my life.
I smile and know love with its endless light.

I smile for each day and all it can bring.
I smile in my heart where true love sings.
I smile for the chance to begin brand new.
I smile for the ways to know love's truth.

Hero's we've seen, Lover's we've been.
Yes wisdom has come from playing love's drum.

I smile for this time that's here on Earth.
I smile as we take this grand rebirth.
I smile just because it feels so right,
As we open again to dance in love's light.

Yes I smile for the friends who've stood by me
I smile for the light in all that I see.
I smile for the Grace that fills up my life.
I smile and know love with its endless delights.

Epilogue …

There are many complicated esoteric practices and thought flows in our world, yet what we have presented here is enough, if applied, to transform each person's life into one that is filled with Grace and gratitude; and also transform our world into one that cares for and honours, all life.

With love, light and laughter,
Jasmuheen

Additional Data:-
For more data on living physically nourished via our Essence energy go to
http://www.jasmuheen.com/living-on-light/

You may also enjoy our more in-depth videos on this lifestyle. L.L.P. 1 – Meditation Magic; plus L.L.P. 2 – Prayer; L.L.P. 3 – programming & mind mastery – Part 1; Part 2; L.L.P. 4 – vegetarianism click here plus Parts 5 to 8 of the above Lifestyle – using exercise, service, silence and song; this last video also shares the benefits of this lifestyle.

JASMUHEEN

- Ambassador of Peace, founder – Embassy of Peace, international lecturer & Online Course facilitator.
- Artist & Sacred Art Retreat facilitator; film-maker & musician.
- Author & metaphysical researcher of 35 books in 18 languages plus Jasmuheen's guided meditations for improving health & happiness. Also enjoy her Successful Living tips in the Our Selves page of our sister site the C.I.A.
- Jasmuheen's Background; Darkroom Training facilitator.
- Researcher into Pranic Living plus living on light and the breatharian agenda.
- President of the Global Congress of Spiritual Scientists – Bangalore, India; Self Empowerment Academy founder & Cosmic Internet Academy facilitator.

Jasmuheen's main service agenda is the
raising of consciousness to co-create
a healthy, harmonious world.

www.jasmuheen.com

http://www.youtube.com/jasmuheen
http://www.facebook.com/pages/Jasmuheen/187152512352

17-18 OUR ESSENCE ≠ P.34 (Baseline)
  18. Great Central ☉ ⎡ The Force That Breathes us P.47
                       ⎢ LOVE
                       ⎣ 41) DNA

63 - No Death

Personality Self = Beta P. 20